TURN OF THE CENTURY STYLE

home decoration and furnishings between 1890 and 1910

PUBLISHED BY MIDDLESEX UNIVERSITY PRESS

CONTENTS

INTRODUCTION

The turn of the century in Britain was a time of rapidly increasing wealth and expansion of the middle classes. People set out to demonstrate their status through their houses, making home decoration an important issue. Due to falling prices, homemakers could afford to buy the plentiful furniture and furnishings available from specialist retailers and the still relatively new department stores.

New houses in late-Victorian towns were generally terraced and built of red brick with steeply pitched slate roofs and sash windows in angular bays. Interiors were designed to impress and were filled with furniture, dense patterns, lavish drapery, plants and numerous decorative ornaments.

By the 1900s, a new style of house was emerging. Semi-detached, with a rounded bay, small-paned casement windows and a low, sloping tiled roof, these houses were influenced by the vernacular style of Arts-and-Crafts

BADDA 302

*Catalogue for Wallace King, about 1909
Turn-of-the-century rooms often included a large
fireplace with an overmantel. Window treatments
became simpler. Turkey rugs continued to be widely
available. The popularity of eighteenth-century
reproductions can be seen in this dining-room furniture
and plasterwork frieze.*

BADDA 1068

architects. Simpler interiors were becoming fashionable. The most up-to-date furniture and furnishings were practical and attractive.

Creating a healthy home environment was considered to be important. Reduced amounts of furniture, fabrics and ornaments meant less dust. More space and moveable floorcoverings made cleaning easier. Rooms were more informal and decorated in light, clear colours. The home was furnished for living rather than primarily to receive visitors.

In the 1900s, several styles of furniture and furnishings were available. As well as Arts-and-Crafts-inspired pieces, some had simplified, elongated motifs, today called Art Nouveau. Historical styles were on sale to create an eighteenth-century look. Chintz and other traditional patterns did not disappear entirely and became popular in the latter part of the period. But many homes continued to look much as they had in the 1890s.

TURN OF THE CENTURY STYLE reflects what was produced and marketed to middle-class consumers to decorate and furnish their homes. Almost all its illustrations are taken from MoDA's collections from this period. It aims to encourage readers to be as interested in home decoration as were the original occupiers of Britain's late-Victorian and Edwardian homes

WALLS AND PAINT

Wall decoration is central to turn-of-the-century style. Popular wall colours altered significantly in this period from dark to light. Dark colour schemes were designed to create the rich, enclosed atmosphere that characterised late-Victorian houses. They also helped to hide dirt generated by coal fires and gas lamps. By the early years of the twentieth century, living rooms and bedrooms were lighter and brighter. However, halls and dining rooms were still often decorated in darker colours.

At the beginning of the period, walls were strongly patterned. In dining rooms and hallways, in particular, they were often divided into three distinct horizontal areas separated by a dado rail and a picture rail. The lowest part of the wall, from the skirting to about waist height, was the dado. Above this, to the picture rail, was the filling. Finally, up to the cornice, was the frieze. Different but co-ordinating patterns were used for each section. The closer they were to the ceiling, the lighter, freer and larger-scale the

patterns became.

With the move towards less highly decorated schemes, this arrangement fell out of fashion. Many early-twentieth-century homes reduced the pattern and colour in a room by enlarging the frieze and dispensing with the dado. The frieze was sometimes the only wall pattern.

There was a marked shift in pattern over the period. Initially, large stylised, often floral motifs, similar to those of William Morris were popular. Later, more restrained and spacious Arts-and-Crafts effects, some with characteristic stylised roses, became prominent. At the same time chintzes and stripes were also available. Garden flower and ribbon patterns were often used in drawing rooms and bedrooms, frequently with Sheraton-style furniture.

Internal woodwork could be either dark or pale. Graining to resemble woods such as mahogany, oak or walnut was widespread. However, white painted woodwork was favoured in paler interiors.

Reproduced by permission of English Heritage, NMR

ILLUSTRATION 1

Drawing room in Moseley, Birmingham, 1890

ILLUSTRATION 1 At the start of the period, walls were densely patterned with co-ordinating papers. Dining-room and hall walls were usually divided into three, while elsewhere in the house, such as the drawing room, it was usual to have a filling paper and frieze. This Birmingham drawing room has two William Morris wallpapers and a William Morris carpet. The tasselled upholstery and profusion of furnishings, ornaments and stylised patterns are typical of late-Victorian taste. Large overmantels and white woodwork were popular from the 1890s and help to date this room.

ILLUSTRATION 2
C & C Wallpaper Pattern Book, 1891

BADDA 2042

BADDA 2042

ILLUSTRATION 2 In the 1890s 'sanitary' papers were widely used particularly in halls, kitchens and attic rooms but they were much less popular by the early years of the twentieth century. Such papers were printed in oil-based inks and varnished, producing a washable surface. They were often used to dado height, an area susceptible to particularly hard wear, but were also available as filling and frieze papers. This is a dado pattern.

ILLUSTRATION 3 Floral papers in blues and pinks were produced for bedrooms. They often covered the entire wall, sometimes with a frieze above. Similar naturalistic floral patterns had been sold for many years and continued to be popular.

ILLUSTRATION 3
C & C Wallpaper Pattern Book, 1891

ILLUSTRATION 4

Alfred Chapman & Co Wallpaper Pattern Book, 1895

ILLUSTRATION 4 Some wallpaper patterns were very large. A design like this might have been combined with a co-ordinated frieze. This sort of stylisation was influenced by the work of the designers William Morris and CFA Voysey. The poppy was a very popular motif in late-nineteenth-century wallpapers but by the early 1900s this was no longer the case.

SW 77

ILLUSTRATION 5

Heffer Scott wallpaper, about 1900

ILLUSTRATION 5 Exaggerated stems and stylised roses are typical of the patterns popular in the early twentieth century. Today we would call them Art Nouveau. Greens, pale mauves and pinks were fashionable. The dark overall effect of this paper suggests it was for a dining room, a space that continued to be decorated in darker colours even in houses where lighter rooms were preferred.

ILLUSTRATION 6 Wallpaper was much more widely chosen for reception rooms than paint. Plain coloured papers were an option. Distemper, a coloured limewash that creates a soft, powdery finish, was sometimes used, generally in pale colours. Emulsion had yet to be invented. Matt oil paint, which was washable, was frequently preferred for kitchen walls and near staircases, areas that were likely to receive a lot of wear. The darker colours in this paint chart were for internal woodwork and the exterior of the house.

ILLUSTRATION 6

Carson's Paint Chart, 1904

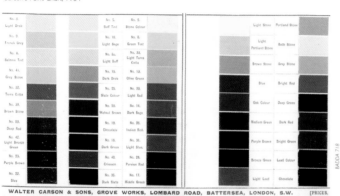

BADDA 7/8

BADDA 929.292

ILLUSTRATION 7

Catalogue for John Line and Sons, 1910

ILLUSTRATION 7 Special papers with pictorial images suitable for children were produced for nurseries throughout the period. Here a Dutch farmyard scene is evoked in simplified, flattened motifs.

BADDA 126.1

Hand-worked Friezes.

10½ inches wide. THE "HANOVER" FRIEZE. No. B 8348, at **1/-** per yard.

10½ inches wide. THE "ROSE BUD" FRIEZE. No. B 8363, at **9d.** per yard.

ILLUSTRATION 8 This page indicates the variety of friezes available in the early twentieth century. Some would continue the theme of the main paper while others adopted an entirely different motif. Landscape scenes and stylised flowers were used in many designs at the time.

ILLUSTRATION 9 A light-coloured paper with a chintz pattern like this might have been used in drawing rooms and bedrooms.

10½ inches wide. THE "VERNON" FRIEZE. No. B 8378, at **1/-** per yard.

10½ inches wide. THE "WROXHAM" FRIEZE. Repeats at about 6 feet 6 inches. No. B/8356, at **1/-** per yard.

ILLUSTRATION 8

Sanderson wallpaper, 1911

ILLUSTRATION 9

Sanderson wallpaper, 1911

BADDA J2907

ILLUSTRATION 10 This east London living room, photographed in 1913, has light walls. It shows the use of a low frieze, here with co-ordinating garden flower and ribbon patterns. In addition note the lace curtains, large tiled fireplace, mirrored overmantel and flower-shaped triple pendant electric light.

ILLUSTRATION 10
Living room in a Leytonstone house, 1913

FLOORING

Choices about flooring, like many other aspects of turn-of-the-century interiors, were partly affected by the need to keep the home clean. Rugs, carpets and runners that could be taken up and beaten were used in preference to fitted carpets.

Large-bordered, patterned carpets were widely available to suit all tastes. They included oriental, classical-revival and Arts-and-Crafts-inspired designs. Patterns were designed to complement wallcoverings and fabrics. Large Turkey rugs in red, green and blue were popular for dining rooms; they deadened the noise of eating and servants' footsteps. Small carpets were produced too. Several might be used in Arts-and-Crafts-style drawing rooms and in hallways on wooden floors.

In the living room, the wooden floor was usually visible around the edge of the carpet. Parquet flooring was desirable. It was available in many elaborate patterns but was expensive. Exposed floorboards were either painted or stained, varnished and polished. Dark brown was a popular colour.

Floorcloth was cheaper than carpet. It was available in two forms – oilcloth, a painted canvas, and the thicker new flooring material, linoleum. Both were popular, being hardwearing and produced to resemble woven carpets, parquet flooring and tiling. The less well off used floorcloth in living rooms instead of carpets. For many it was a practical choice for bedrooms, kitchens and bathrooms. Linoleum, with washable rugs on top, was also suitable for nurseries.

Ceramic floor tiles were used in some kitchens and bathrooms and in many hallways in the earlier part of the period. Similar geometrically tiled paths often led from the gate up to the front door. Small moulded tiles, which imitated mosaic pavements, were another, but much more expensive, option for hallways. Matting or a carpet strip, laid on plain polished wooden hall floors, was a much cheaper alternative.

ILLUSTRATION I

Carpet designs by Arthur Silver, 1894

ILLUSTRATION I Carpets were generally rectangular with a distinct border. These designs are for a carpet border and 'filling'. The colours and pattern are typical of the 1890s.

ILLUSTRATION 2 The Arts and Crafts designer, CFA Voysey used completely flattened, simplified floral forms. This carpet filling is an example of his patterns for flooring. His fabrics and wallpapers often had similar designs.

ILLUSTRATION 3 Geometrically tiled hallway floors were popular until about 1905. They were decorative and easy to clean. Patterns were put together from tiles that came in standard square, triangular, octagonal and hexagonal pieces. Border tiles were needed around the edge to complete the overall design. Such flooring was complex to lay and expensive.

ILLUSTRATION 2

Carpet by CFA Voysey, about 1898

DOULTON, & Co.,

CROWN WHARF, GROVE ROAD, VICTORIA PARK, LONDON, E.,

MANUFACTURERS & MERCHANTS.

ENCAUSTIC AND TESSELATED TILES,
PLAIN & ORNAMENTAL WALL TILES, BOTH ENGLISH & FOREIGN
TILES FOR HEARTHS, WINDOW BOXES & FURNITURE.
ART DECORATED TILES TO ORDER.

SCALE 1 INCH TO A FOOT

ORNAMENTAL BUILDING GOODS OF EVERY DESCRIPTION
LIMES, CEMENTS, PLASTERS, FIRE GOODS, CUTTERS & BUILDING BRICKS
PRICES ON APPLICATION

ILLUSTRATION 3
Catalogue for Doulton's, about 1900

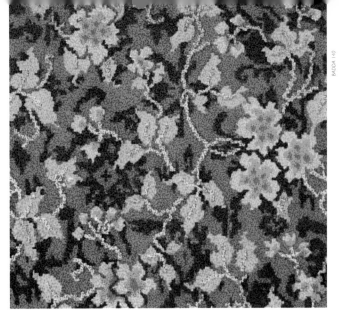

BADDA 140

ILLUSTRATION 4

Catalogue for Green & Edwards, 1905

ILLUSTRATION 5

Catalogue for Barry, Ostlere & Shepherd, about 1900

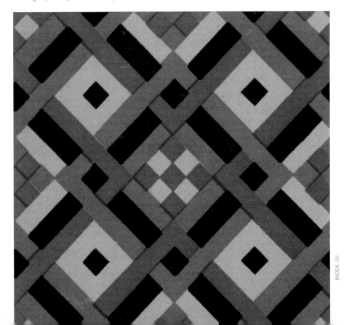

BADDA 101

ILLUSTRATION 4 This floral linoleum pattern might have been used in a living room. Similar designs for both carpet and linoleum had been produced for some time and continued for years to come.

ILLUSTRATION 5 For those who could not afford wooden parquet flooring, imitation parquet linoleum was available. It was suitable for living and dining rooms and hallways.

ILLUSTRATION 6

Catalogue for Waring's, about 1910

BADDA 148

ILLUSTRATION 6 The movement away from fitted carpets led to the widespread use of large rugs on polished or stained wooden floorboards. Deep red, green and blue Turkey rugs had been available for many years and were still popular, particularly in dining rooms.

ILLUSTRATION 7

ILLUSTRATION 7
The Book of the Home, vol I, by HC Davidson, 1906

ILLUSTRATION 8

Catalogue for Williamson
& Cole's about 1908

THE "ORIGINAL" ROMAN ART CARPET.
Moss Rose and Fern Design.   Colour 0216.

This square can be supplied in almost any shade.

THE "ORIGINAL" ROMAN ART CARPET.
The Rose and Bow Design.   Colour 1488.
As recommended by Mrs. Talbot Coke.

This Carpet supplied in almost any shade.

ILLUSTRATION 7 A hardwearing covering that was easy to clean was needed on the staircase. Floorcloth was one option. Like carpet, it was laid as a runner with stair rods. Many patterns were available, including Turkey carpet designs.

ILLUSTRATION 8 Bordered carpets, sold in a range of sizes. These colours were typical of the 1900s. Both pattern and colour would have gone well with striped or floral wallpaper.

FURNITURE

By today's standards most middle-class late-nineteenth-century rooms contained a lot of furniture. Standard items included a settee and easy chairs, several upright chairs and small occasional tables, a bureau, a china cabinet, a screen, a piano and music stool, and perhaps card and sewing tables. However, some people were starting to cut down, influenced partly by the desire to make cleaning easier, an increasing turn-of-the-century preoccupation. But, with the expanding middle classes keen to demonstrate their improvement in status, most homes still had an immaculately furnished drawing room, kept for visitors and special occasions.

Built-in furniture addressed the desire for cleanliness in the home by reducing dust-traps. It had the additional advantage of utilising limited space, particularly around the edges of a room. Inglenooks and 'cosy corners', arches and screens, were all popular options to define and divide spaces. Fitted furniture was produced for bedrooms and kitchens, where hygiene was a particular concern.

All furniture was available in a wide range of styles from the historic to the more contemporary. The latter was strongly influenced by the ideas of William Morris and the Arts and Crafts Movement. Made from English woods and clearly showing its construction, Arts-and-Crafts-inspired furniture could be natural, stained or plainly painted. Reproduction styles were also popular and included designs based on Queen Anne, Sheraton and Chippendale furniture. Manufacturers produced suites suitable for the different rooms.

At the beginning of the period, seating was generally rather upright and tightly upholstered. In the living room, a settee or chesterfield was generally placed at right angles to the fireplace. There would be one or two matching easy chairs and several upright chairs. But by 1910, in keeping with the generally more relaxed atmosphere in the home, less formal and more comfortable-looking armchairs were widely available.

Wm. Wallace & Co's Inexpensive Artistic Boudoir Furniture.

AN • ARTISTIC • DRAWING-ROOM.

It is almost impossible to give the exact cost of decorating and furnishing a room as illustrated above, without knowing the size and shape, but WM. WALLACE & CO. will be pleased to give an estimate, free of cost, for completely furnishing and decorating, and will submit patterns of Wall-Papers, in all the newest styles and colourings—many of these are registered designs, and can only be obtained at WM. WALLACE & CO.'S—also prices for any of the above articles upon receipt of particulars. WM. WALLACE & CO. invite special attention to their Window Curtains with brocade and plush valances; these curtains are inexpensive, and are made in a great variety of materials, and are strongly recommended by Mrs. Panton, Mrs. Talbot Coke, and Miss Charlotte Robinson, the well-known authorities on Artistic Home Decoration and Furnishing.

ILLUSTRATION I

Catalogue for William Wallace & Co, about 1895

ILLUSTRATION I 'Cosy corners', usually including two high-backed settees placed at right angles with shelves above, could be built into drawing rooms. They were particularly useful where space was limited, combining several functions in one piece. Creating a place to relax alone or with family and friends, they could also be used to divide up a room. Portable screens and furniture arranged in groups also helped to define areas. Fireplaces with large, mirrored overmantels were a prominent feature. Numerous small tables were dotted around, some of them supporting the popular palms and house plants.

ILLUSTRATION 2
Catalogue for Oetzmann's, about 1890

BADDA 1/64

Solid oak or walnut Piano, with gilt incised panel, and two candelabra, a well-made and thoroughly sound instrument, well adapted for hard wear .. .. ,, 29 Guineas.

Handsome walnut Piano with inlaid panel, brass candle sconces, iron frame, trichord, check action, ivory keys, and all the latest improvements .. .. ,, 27 Guineas.

ILLUSTRATION 2 A piano was essential for entertaining the family and guests. They were available in many different styles and were selected to blend in with living-room furniture. Late Victorians draped their pianos with fabrics, as they did their doors and windows. This fashion was on the wane by the early years of the twentieth century.

ILLUSTRATION 3 Furniture was sold in suites for drawing rooms, dining rooms and bedrooms. This tapestry-upholstered walnut drawing-room suite comprises a couch, two types of easy chair and upright chairs.

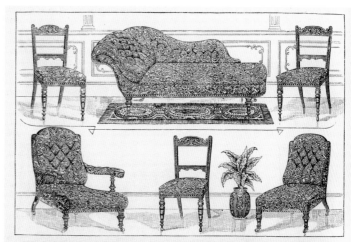

BADDA 1/64

ILLUSTRATION 3
Catalogue for Oetzmann's, about 1890

Solid walnut Suite, comprising comfortable Couch, Lounge, Easy Chair and Lady's comfortable Chair, and four Chairs, well upholstered and covered with tapestry £8 15 0

ILLUSTRATION 4
The British Home of To-day, edited by W Shaw Sparrow, 1904

ILLUSTRATION 4 Arts-and-Crafts furniture made of light-coloured wood, such as native oak and sycamore, was designed to show how it was constructed. This English oak dining table, by the designer and craftsman Sydney Barnsley, is typical. Such furniture was expensive and was sold by shops such as Heal's and Liberty & Co, leading retailers of modern designs.

ILLUSTRATION 5
Catalogue for Williamsonson & Cole's, about 1908

ILLUSTRATION 5 In the early twentieth century, easy chairs became more substantial. These are upholstered in traditional tapestry or in Arts-and-Crafts designs.

ILLUSTRATION 6 By 1910, there was a move towards more comfortable furniture and more naturalistic patterning. Well-padded upholstered easy chairs were available with loose covers, such as these with their traditional chintz fabric.

ILLUSTRATION 6

Catalogue for Williamsonson & Cole's, about 1908

Loose Covers

SPECIALISTS

FOR

Loose Covers,
Casement Blinds,
Bordered
Curtains,
Etc.

The Welbeck Chair.
With Loose Cover of Fête de Roses Cretonne.

The "Lonsdale" Chair.
With Loose Cover of " Rose Rambler " printed
Linen or Glaced Chintz fast Colours.

EXPERIENCED CUTTERS
SENT TO ALL PARTS OF
THE UNITED KINGDOM
FIT GUARANTEED

Estimates Free

CHARGES for MAKING		
Prices for making Loose Covers, unlined and unflounced—		
Small Chairs ... from	1/6
Lady's Easy Chair „	3/6
Gent's Easy... ... „	4/6
Chesterfields ... „	7/6

8007

The "Cromwell" Chair.
With Loose Cover of Shadow Rose Cretonne or
Glazed Chintz, with Blue or Green Ribbon.

The Luxurious Divan Chair.
With Loose Cover of Amara Chintz or Taffeta.

cw. H. 113080, col. orig.

ILLUSTRATION 7

Catalogue for Waring's, about 1910

18/6 Oak Dining Chair with strong under-framing Seat, covered in Tapestry.

10/18/6 Oak Side-board, 5′ 6″ in length. Antique copper fittings, repousse panel in centre of lower part.

1/16/6 Oak Carving Chair to match.

BADDA 148

ILLUSTRATION 8

The Book of the Home, vol III, by HC Davidson, 1906

BADDA 1036

ILLUSTRATION 7 Suites of dining furniture included dining chairs, a table and a large sideboard. Easy chairs, a bookcase and desk were also sometimes placed in the room. This Arts-and-Crafts-style oak sideboard has a decorative copper repoussé panel and copper fittings. The chairs are covered in tapestry.

ILLUSTRATION 8 This early 1900s bedroom by Liberty & Co has a built-in wardrobe, cupboards and tiled washstand. Fabric is hung on the wall behind the bed and there is similar strong patterning to the walls. The contrasting white woodwork adds a fresh look to the room. Bedrooms were often given a floral feminine treatment. Metal bedsteads, due to their smooth, shiny surfaces, were thought to be more hygienic than wood, in which bugs might live. Bed draperies had been widely used but for similar reasons were by 1906 much reduced.

ILLUSTRATION 9 Bedrooms were generally light, airy and less expensively furnished than reception rooms. Cane seats were an alternative to heavier upholstered chairs. Most houses, including those with bathrooms, had a washstand in each bedroom. Made of wood, they usually had a hygienic marble top and tiled splashback.

ILLUSTRATION 9
Catalogue for Waring's, about 1910

ILLUSTRATION 10

Catalogue for Waring's, about 1910

ILLUSTRATION 10 This Edwardian drawing room is light and uncluttered. This effect results partly from the pale colours and simple patterns. The compact eighteenth-century-style seating, with its tight-fitting silk covers also contributes. The inlaid mahogany furniture includes a china cabinet. Other decorative objects are displayed in the 'cosy corners' on either side of the fireplace.

CURTAINS AND UPHOLSTERY

Complex arrangements of curtains, blinds and other forms of shading, such as stained glass screens, were still popular at the end of the nineteenth century. Drapery and upholstery were frequently trimmed with braids, tassels and embroidered bands. Ornate window dressings had been developed to provide privacy, protect furnishings from the sun and to make an impressive display.

Blinds were much used inside and out. Indoors they were hung next to the window, behind lace and dress curtains. Options included venetian, festoon and roller blinds.

However, heavy drapery collected dust and, as concerns switched to keeping the house clean, simpler window treatments became popular. These suited the casement windows of the new twentieth-century houses with their smaller panes and leaded glass. Curtains hung straight from a pole or rail. Their tops were folded back over the rail to create a trim or there would often be a gathered valance.

Chairs were generally upholstered with tight-fitting, fixed woven covers, embellished with studs or fringing. They could have removable loose covers to protect furniture from coal dust and sunshine. In the 1900s, more comfortable easy chairs with loose covers, often made of chintz, became available.

Fabrics came in many patterns throughout the period. Naturalistic designs were always offered, but there were many more two-dimensional 'flat' patterns that did not copy nature directly. These included Arts-and-Crafts textiles inspired by those of William Morris. More stylised still were the sinuous flowers and organic curving leaves that emerged in the 1890s, in the style known today as Art Nouveau. Such designs were overtaken in popularity by plainer and more traditional patterns in the first decade of the twentieth century, when chintz and late-eighteenth-century motifs experienced a revival.

ILLUSTRATION 1

Catalogue for Oetzmann's, about 1890

INSIDE BLINDS.

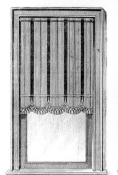

WOVEN LINEN FANCY STRIPED BLINDS
On Wood Rollers with Brass Furniture, Tassels and
Cord complete, 4½d. per square foot.
Ditto on best Spring Rollers, 6½d. per square foot.
On Customer's own Rollers 3d. per square foot.
Shaped Valances trimmed with Fringe and Lace,
from 6d. per foot run of the width.

FESTOON BLINDS
In Madras Muslins, Indian Printed Cottons, Sateens,
Indian Brocades or Striped Silk, Art-Coloured
Indian or China Silks, from 1/6 per square foot.

Patterns and Estimates Free on Application.

VENETIAN BLINDS
Dull or Varnished Colors, with Strong Duck Web-
and Cord, 6d. per square foot.
Superior qualities, Varnished or Dull Colors or Varnished imitation of any wood, 7d., 8d. and 9d. per
square foot.
Special quality, strongly recommended, 10d. per square
foot.
Patent Check Action 1d. per foot extra.
Old Venetian Blinds Washed, Retaped and new Cords
from 2½d. per square foot.
Old Venetian Blinds Repainted, Retaped and new Cords
from 4d. per square foot.

Blinds containing less than 16 square feet charged as 16 square feet.

PATTERNS AND ESTIMATES FREE ON APPLICATION.

ILLUSTRATION 2

Catalogue for Oetzmann's, about 1890

ILLUSTRATION 1 Large bays with sash windows were the height of respectability in the late nineteenth century. Patterned lace or muslin curtains were used in virtually all houses at this time. Heavier curtains with swags and elaborate braiding and fringes were often hung on top.

ILLUSTRATION 2 Internal blinds were widespread in the 1890s. Fabric roller and festoon blinds were finished with various trimmings. They were made in muslins, cottons, sateens, brocades and silks. Venetian blinds were generally wooden and might be stained, varnished or painted. They were also available in glass and iron.

BADDA 2027

ILLUSTRATION 3

Catalogue for Williamson & Cole's, about 1908

ILLUSTRATION 4

Catalogue for Williamson & Cole's, about 1908

Cornice Poles and Fittings

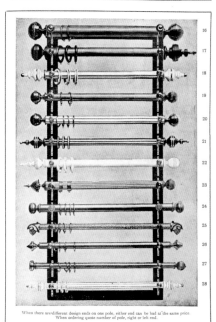

16
17
18
19
20
21
22
23
24
25
26
27
28

When there are different design ends on one pole, either end can be had at the same price.
When ordering quote number of pole, right or left end.

BADDA 2027

ILLUSTRATION 3 In the early twentieth century, elaborate drapery was replaced by simpler arrangements. Short, lightweight casement blinds were hung next to the panes and drawn as needed to protect furnishings from sunlight while still letting in light. Thicker, floor-length curtains were made either from a plain fabric with an appliquéd border, or a patterned fabric combined with a plain toning border.

ILLUSTRATION 4 Lace and dress curtains were hung from sturdy curtain poles with decorative finials. Poles were produced in different finishes including natural and painted woods, brass and antique copper.

ST 323

ILLUSTRATION 5
Textile designed by the Silver Studio, about 1895

ILLUSTRATION 5 Printed cottons and linens were used for curtains, cushions and loose covers. This example shows the influence of William Morris.

ILLUSTRATION 6 Throughout this period, sturdy woven fabrics with unobtrusive motifs remained popular for upholstery.

ILLUSTRATION 7 Woven silks and brocades were fashionable for upholstering late-eighteenth-century-style furniture particularly in urban homes. This French-manufactured silk, with its elegant Art Nouveau pattern, would have been considered suitable for Sheraton-style furniture.

ILLUSTRATION 6
Textile, about 1905

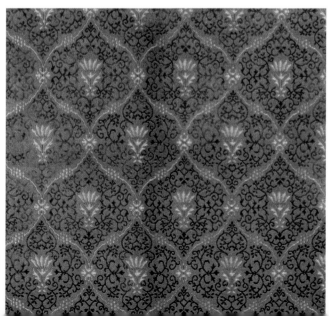

ST 949

ILLUSTRATION 7

Textile designed by the Silver Studio, 1898

ST 955

ILLUSTRATION 8

Textile designed by the Silver Studio, about 1905

ILLUSTRATION 8 Tapestry fabrics were often used for upholstery. This early-twentieth-century example has a typical 'Jacobean' embroidery pattern. The modern, Morris-influenced patterns of the late nineteenth century were beginning to go out of fashion by this date.

ILLUSTRATION 9 Chintz patterns, often featuring roses and ribbons and usually in pale greens, creams, pinks and blues, were very popular in the early twentieth century. This example was probably used for curtains or loose covers.

ST 956

ILLUSTRATION 9

Textile manufactured by GP & J Baker, about 1905

FIREPLACES AND HEATING

Coal fires were universal at this period, though gas and electric models were available. There were fireplaces in all reception rooms and smaller, plainer versions in bedrooms. In the drawing room the fireplace was the focal decorative feature, positioned centrally on a long wall.

At the start of the period, mantelpieces were wider than they were high. They were often draped with fabrics, fringes and tassels. Such ornament was in keeping with the lavish dress curtains and other elaborate draperies. This also allowed older fireplaces to look up-to-date.

By 1900, under the influence of the Arts and Crafts movement and reproduction furniture styles, undraped wooden mantels were most desirable. Characteristically vertical, early-twentieth-century fireplaces usually extended almost to the height of the picture rail. The vertical was emphasised through the addition of columns and pilasters to the overmantel. The fireplace was topped off with a wide horizontal shelf, often used to display ornaments and family pictures.

Many fires included an integral overmantel with a central mirror and shelves or a glass-fronted cabinet on either side. Overmantels were either finished as polished natural woods or painted white. They took up a lot of wall space and dominated many rooms.

Tiled surrounds were popular. As the period progressed, plain coloured tiles were increasingly preferred to patterns. Hearths and curbs could also be tiled with sturdier, plain or simple block-printed patterns. A hearth rug was indispensable, as were fire irons.

'Cosy corners' or inglenooks, fitted into the recesses on either side of the protruding chimneybreast, were popular. The hall of a newly built, large Edwardian house was wide and treated as a room rather than a passageway. It might include a small fireplace surrounded by inglenook seating.

ILLUSTRATION I

Catalogue for O'Brien, Thomas & Co, 1893

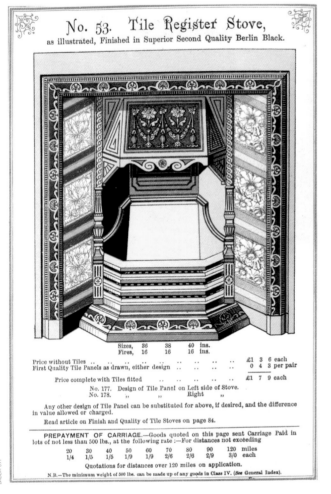

No. 53. Tile Register Stove,
as illustrated, Finished in Superior Second Quality Berlin Black.

Sizes,	36	38	40	ins.
Fires,	16	16	16	ins.

Price without Tiles .. .. £1 3 6 each
First Quality Tile Panels as drawn, either design .. .. 0 4 3 per pair

Price complete with Tiles fitted .. .. £1 7 9 each

No. 177. Design of Tile Panel on Left side of Stove.
No. 178. „ „ „ Right „

Any other design of Tile Panel can be substituted for above, if desired, and the difference in value allowed or charged.

Read article on Finish and Quality of Tile Stoves on page 84.

PREPAYMENT OF CARRIAGE.—Goods quoted on this page sent Carriage Paid in lots of not less than 500 lbs., at the following rate :—For distances not exceeding

20	30	40	50	60	70	80	90	120 miles
1/4	1/5	1/5	1/9	1/9	2/6	2/6	2/9	3/0 each

Quotations for distances over 120 miles on application.

N.B.—The minimum weight of 500 lbs. can be made up of any goods in Class IV. (*See* General Index.)

BADDA 697

ILLUSTRATION I Late-nineteenth-century cast-iron grates often had a narrow vertical opening with a canopy hood and splayed cheeks to improve their efficiency. Reception-room fireplaces were usually decorated with colourful patterned tiles, which were available in a huge variety of designs. Fireplaces in less public rooms – bedrooms and nurseries for example – were smaller and of less note.

ILLUSTRATION 2 Elaborate overmantels with shelves, a mirror and perhaps glass-fronted cupboards were very popular by 1890. Some were in historic designs to co-ordinate with the furniture. Produced in a range of woods, some included painted panels.

ILLUSTRATION 3 Mantel boards and draperies were much used in the late nineteenth century, either to disguise an unfortunate fireplace or simply to make an important decorative feature.

Handsome walnut or black and gold Glass, with decorated panel with bevelled plates, 4 ft. high by 4 ft. wide ... £3 17 6
(If without gilding and with top panel glass, 5s. less.)

Walnut, oak or mahogany Overmantel, nicely carved and with six bevelled edge glass plates, 4 ft. 9 in. wide by 4 ft. high ... £3 3 0

ILLUSTRATION 2
Catalogue for Oetzmann's, about 1890

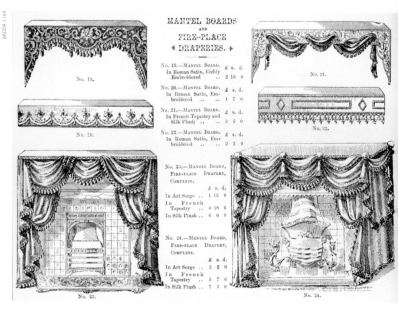

ILLUSTRATION 3
Catalogue for Oetzmann's, about 1890

Real Wolf Skin, mounted on Black Goat, 42s., 52s. 6d., 63s., 84s.

Real Bear Skin, mounted on Black Goat, 84s., 95s., 115s., 147s.

Real Bear Skin, mounted on Bear, 8 guineas to 15 guineas.

ILLUSTRATION 4
Catalogue for Oetzmann's, about 1890

ILLUSTRATION 4 Rectangular hearth rugs were often used in front of fireplaces. Many were made of sheepskin or real fur which, unlike today, was then quite acceptable.

ILLUSTRATION 5 A coal scuttle and fire irons were needed in every home. The fire irons were displayed in a formal arrangement with their handles resting on the fender.

ILLUSTRATION 6 Fenders were essential to protect the carpet from spitting coal. These late-nineteenth-century examples in steel and brass are highly decorated.

ILLUSTRATION 5
Catalogue for Adshead & Smellie, 1897

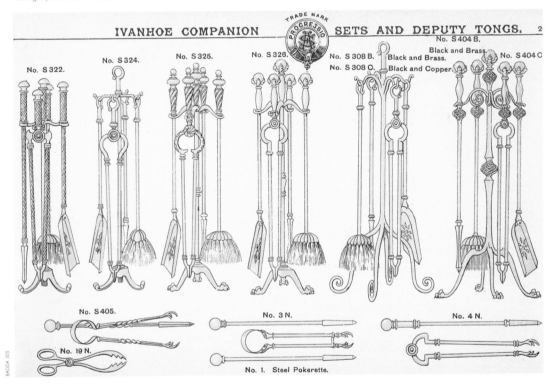

IVANHOE COMPANION SETS AND DEPUTY TONGS. 2

No. S 322.

No. S 324.

No. S 325.

No. S 326.

TRADE MARK
PROGRESSIO

No. S 308 B. Black and Brass.
No. S 308 C. Black and Copper.

No. S 404 B.
Black and Brass.
No. S 404 C

No. S 405.

No. 19 N.

No. 3 N.

No. 1. Steel Pokerette.

No. 4 N.

BADDA 305

ILLUSTRATION 6

Catalogue for Adshead & Smellie, 1897

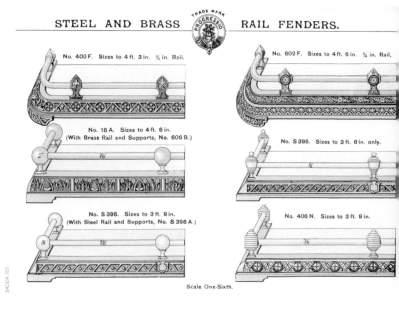

STEEL AND BRASS RAIL FENDERS.

No. 400 F. Sizes to 4 ft. 3 in. ⅝ in. Rail.

No. 602 F. Sizes to 4 ft. 6 in. ¾ in. Rail.

No. 18 A. Sizes to 4 ft. 6 in.
(With Brass Rail and Supports, No. 606 B.)

No. S 395. Sizes to 3 ft. 6 in. only.

No. S 396. Sizes to 3 ft. 9 in.
(With Steel Rail and Supports, No. S 396 A.)

No. 406 N. Sizes to 3 ft. 9 in.

Scale One-Sixth.

ILLUSTRATION 7 This fireplace at the home of the architect, CFA Voysey, is in the high Arts-and-Crafts style of the turn of the century. It is taller than it is wide, with a flat front and plain tiles. Less extreme versions became commercially available in the early twentieth century.

ILLUSTRATION 8
Catalogue for Mallet & Son, about 1905

ILLUSTRATION 8 Although Arts-and-Crafts mantelpieces were usually wooden, this one is in cast iron. It does, however, have the typical vertical shape and plain tiling as well as Art Nouveau motifs.

ILLUSTRATION 9 The drawing room fireplace in this extensive early 1900s house is tiled and has a large mirrored overmantel on which many decorative objects are displayed. The fire has a brass fender and there is a firescreen. While the overall lightness of the room, electric lighting and comfortable, chintz-covered armchairs are all modern features, the large number of pictures and exotic palm are more typical of the 1890s.

DRAWING ROOM

ILLUSTRATION 9
Drawing room, Barry Island, about 1910

LIGHTING

Most turn-of-the-century middle-class homes had gas lighting. Electricity for domestic use had been introduced in 1882, but it was not available everywhere and local suppliers would provide electricity only to households in areas where they believed bills would be paid. Although many newly built houses in the 1900s were wired for electricity, overall they were still in a minority. Even by 1918 only six per cent of British homes were so equipped. Electric lighting was a major selling point and was highlighted in sales advertisements. More expensive than gas, it was an indicator of social status. People also used oil lamps, either as the main source of lighting or to supplement gas or electricity.

Gas was convenient and efficient compared to candles or oil, emitting more than five times the light, but it gave out dirty fumes that blackened rooms and their contents. It was thought to be unhealthy as bedroom lighting. Halls were the one area of the house where gas lighting was favoured. Gas was, however, the only option for many people and new types of gas mantles were developed to increase light levels.

Electricity was much cleaner. Its use reduced the need for a major annual spring-clean and regular redecoration. It also stimulated a shift in colour schemes, as pale-coloured walls and fabrics were now practical. Although bulbs were not powerful by today's standards, compared with previous interiors, turn-of-the century rooms seemed light and bright.

Fittings and shades were generally similar for both gas and electricity and there was a wide choice including historic revival, Arts-and-Crafts and Art Nouveau styles. Shades were made from glass, fabric and beads. Some designs for electric lights, particularly flower-shaped glass shades, made a feature of the glass bulb to emphasise the modernity of the energy source.

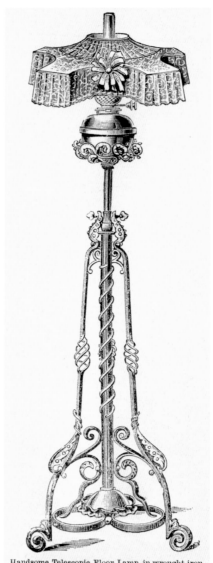

No. 43.
Duplex Lamp, with imitation wrought iron pedestal and copper mounts, richly moulded fount, &c., 11s. 9d.

No. 45.
Handsome Table Lamp, richly hand painted, best duplex burner, with globe ... 27s 6d.
If 50-candle power burner, 32s.6d.

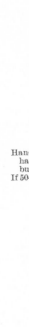

No. 44.
Polished Brass 50-candle power Lamp, complete, 17s. 6d.
If duplex ... ... 12s. 6d.

No. 46.
Brass Pillar Duplex Lamp, with richly cut fount and globe, complete ... ... 21s. 0d.
If Ruby fount ... ... 23s. 9d.

Handsome Telescopic Floor Lamp, in wrought iron, richly relieved with copper scroll work, rising to 7 ft., fitted with opal, engraved or colored globe, &c., in ruby, blue or amber, and lever duplex extinguisher burner, complete ... ... £4 4s.
18 in. Lace Shade (as illustrated), with best brass holder ... ... 10/6 extra.

BADDA 1/64

BADDA 1/64

ILLUSTRATION 1 Oil table lamps were useful and portable. They usually had glass shades.

ILLUSTRATION 2 Frilly fabric lampshades, some with fringes, were used on standard lamps and table lights throughout the period. This is an example of an ornate standard oil lamp from the 1890s.

ILLUSTRATION 3 Chain-hung lanterns were used in halls. Lantern-shaped wall lights were also available. Glass, which was sometimes coloured, was frequently combined with brass. These examples were designed for oil or gas.

ILLUSTRATION 3
Catalogue for Oetzmann's, about 1890

Handsome Hall Lantern for oil, with door, in polished brass and cathedral glass with bevelled centres, fitted with best duplex burner, &c., complete ... 27s. 6d.

Polished Brass Hall Lantern, 11 in. by 7 in., for oil, in cathedral glass,with chains to pull down, chimney, &c. Complete... 13s. 9d. If with rod and door, 10s. 9d.

Polished Brass Gas Hall Lantern, fitted with artistic cathedral stained glass and bevelled centres, 27s. 6d.

Hall Lantern for Gas, amber globe ... 21s. Ruby globe ... 2Fs.

Hall Lantern in polished brass frame, fitted for gas, with rich colored cathedral glass, 21s. 0d. If with bevelled plate glass and cut stars ... ... 25s. 6d.

Baby Oil Lantern, for Landing or Recess, white 5s. 11d. Ruby ... 6s. 11d.

Handsome Hall Lantern for oil, with door, in polished brass and cathedral glass with bevelled centres, fitted with best duplex burner &c., complete ... ... 25s. 6d.

BADDA 1164

ILLUSTRATION 4 Overhead lights often had several shades supported by curved metal arms, whether designed for gas or electricity. Rise-and-fall pendants were frequently used in dining rooms. Some electric pendant lights had exposed bulbs, particularly when used in flower-shaped fittings. WAS Benson's simple, Arts-and-Crafts-inspired light fittings in brass and copper were influential. This Benson electric triple pendant reflected light from the ceiling, creating bright but diffused light.

ILLUSTRATION 4
The British Home of Today, edited by W Shaw Sparrow, 1904

BADDA 2072

Stiff.

$\frac{3}{8}$ × 11-in. Back, 4-in.

G 23198	Polished	.. ..	5/- each.
G 23198a	Steel Bronzed and Relieved,	5/-	,,
G 23198b	Oxidized Copper finish	5/6	,,

ILLUSTRATION 5 Wall lights were recommended in drawing rooms and studies as giving a more pleasant effect than a central pendant. They were fixed to either side of the fireplace on static or moveable brackets. Globe-shaped glass shades with etched glass patterns were widely available for all kinds of lights.

ILLUSTRATION 5
Art & Utility in Gas Fittings, *1911*

Messenger & Sons Patent Silver Plated Duplex Annular and other Lamps.

Silver plating is the best.

English Manufacture throughout.

BACDA 146

C H 2419. Bijou Lamp.
Silver plated on German Silver, 31/6.
C.H. 3854. Hand Printed
Chene Silk Shade.
7 in. dia., 10/-

HARRODS
Ltd.

HARRODS
Ltd.

C H 3489.
Embroidered
Taffeta Silk,
8 in. dia., 6/6

C H 219.

C H 3467.
Hand Printed
Chene Silk Shade,
8 in. dia., 7/9

C H 2409.

C H 432. Table Lamp.
Silver plated on Brass, with Messenger's
Patent Duplex Extinguisher and
Raised Burner, 42/6
(Height to top of burner 19 in.)

Bijou Lamps,
Silver plated on
German Silver.
26/-

Bijou Lamps,
Silver plated on
German Silver.
38/6

C H 285. Table Lamp.
Silver plated on Brass with Messenger's
Patent Duplex Extinguisher and
Raised Burner, 40/-
(Height to top of burner 18 in.).

C H 2893.
Hand Printed Chene Silk Shades.
16   18   20 in.
31/6   36/9   47/6

Our assortment of Shades is the finest
in the kingdom.

C H 2897.
Hand Printed Chene Silk Shades,
16   18   20 in.
31/6   36/9   47/6

Stock comprises the least expensive
to most costly productions.

HARRODS
Ltd.

HARRODS
Ltd.

C H 384.
Table Lamp.
Silver plated on
Brass with
Messenger's
Patent Duplex
Extinguisher and
Raised Burner.
Richly Cut Glass
Container. 35/3

(Height to top of burner 23 in.)

C H 14.
Table Lamp.
Silver Plated on
German Silver,
with Messenger's
Patent Duplex
Extinguisher
and Raised
Burner.
Richly Cut Glass
Container. 89/3

(Height to top of burner 27 in.)

(Height to top of burner 22 in.)

C H 354.
Table Lamp.
Silver Plated on
German Silver,
with Messenger's
Patent Duplex
Extinguisher
and Raised
Burner.
Richly Cut Glass
Container. 63/6

C H 2889.
Hand Printed Chene Silk Shades.
16   18   20   22 in.
23/6   26/9   31/6   36/9

C H 2818.
Hand Printed Chene Silk Shades,
Handsome heavy Silk Fringe,
16 in. 39/6   19 in. 56/-

C H 2884.
Hand Printed Chene Silk Shades.
16   18   20   22 in.
23/6   26/9   31/6   36/9

ILLUSTRATION 6 Colourful lampshades had been available for years. They came in various colours to suit different schemes and were produced for standard, table, wall and desk lights. This selection of rose-and-ribbon-style lamps were sold by the London department store, Harrods.

ILLUSTRATION 6

Catalogue for Harrods, about 1905

FINISHING TOUCHES

The late-Victorian drawing room or parlour was the place where guests were received and was designed to impress. It was often very full, not only with furniture and draperies but with many decorative items – pictures, photographs, ornaments, mirrors, plant stands, jardinières, small tables, screens, work boxes, albums and so on. Natural history was of great interest and glass cases of ferns, aquariums and cabinets of fossils or shells might also be found.

Picture rails, overmantels and other shelving were used for display. Often the walls were so densely hung it was hard to see the wallpaper. Objects were also carefully arranged on small tables, many with lace or velvet coverings, positioned by the sides of chairs and sofas.

This habit continued in many homes well into the twentieth century. However, under the influence of the Arts and Crafts movement, there was a trend towards a more restrained use of decorative items. This was exemplified in William Morris's famous dictum, 'Have nothing in your house which you do not know to be useful and believe to be beautiful'.

The drawing room or parlour continued to be the main place for display but by the 1900s it was becoming less full. Increasingly used as a family space rather than just for special occasions and visitors, its changing function and greater informality was reflected in the new terms 'living room' or 'sitting room'.

Throughout this period, other rooms in had less elaborate schemes. Dining rooms often had pictures on the wall but there were fewer ornaments and small pieces of furniture. A maid usually served meals from a large sideboard so its surface had to be kept relatively clear. Bedrooms were of lower importance and usually contained few ornamental objects, although there would probably have been a washstand holding at least one functional but decorative jug and basin. Other private areas, such as bathrooms and kitchens, were plainer still.

ILLUSTRATION 1

Drawing room, about 1911

SE 18089

ILLUSTRATION 1 Although this photograph was taken in 1911, the room shows many late-Victorian features. The walls are covered with pictures and plates, and the fireplace has a mantelboard drapery. The wallpaper and frieze are the main clues to the later date.

ILLUSTRATION 2 Entertaining was important and the dining table would be carefully arranged with the best china, glass, cutlery and elaborate flower arrangements. Dinner-party food was also expected to look attractive.

ILLUSTRATION 3 In the late nineteenth century, hand-painted Japanese-style folding screens were a popular way of dividing up the living room. Bamboo fire screens were also used. Small tables might support jardinières.

ILLUSTRATION 2

Mrs Beeton's Everyday Cookery and Housekeeping Book, 1890

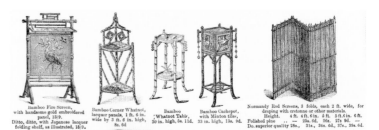

Bamboo Fire Screen,
with handsome gold embroidered
panel, 13/9.
Ditto, ditto, with Japanese lacquer
folding shelf, as illustrated, 15/9.

Bamboo Corner Whatnot,
lacquer panels, 1 ft. 6 in.
wide by 3 ft. 6 in. high,
8s. 6d

Bamboo
Whatnot Table,
30 in. high, 8s. 11d.

Bamboo Cachepot,
with Minton tiles,
33 in. high, 13s. 9d.

Normandy Rod Screens, 3 folds, each 2 ft. wide, for
draping with cretonne or other materials.
Height.   4 ft. 4 ft. 6 in.   5 ft.   5 ft. 6 in.   6 ft.
Polished pine   . . — 25s. 6d.   26s.   27s 9d. —
Do. superior quality 28s.,   31s.,   34s. 6d.,   37s.,   39s. 6d.

ILLUSTRATION 3

Catalogue for Oetzmann's, about 1890

Handsome Japanese Four-fold Screen, 3 ft. 6 in. high by 7 ft. 6 in. wide when open. The
panels richly embroidered with gold . .   . .   14s. 6d.
Superior   ditto   ditto   . .   . .   18s. 9d., 25s. 6d., 37s. 6d. and 45s. 0d.
Ditto,   ditto   4 ft. 6 in. high   . .   . .   . .   9s. 5d., 11s. 9d. and 17s. 6d.

Handsome Japanese Screen, hand-painted, four fold, 4 ft. 6 in.
high, 5s. 6d.
Ditto   5 ft. 6 in. high, opens out to 7 ft. 6 in., 8s. 9d.

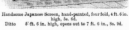

FOR CONDITIONS UNDER WHICH GOODS ARE SENT CARRIAGE PAID PLEASE SEE PAGE 3. ALL CARPETS MADE UP FREE OF CHARGE.

ILLUSTRATION 4

Catalogue for Oetzmann's, about 1890

JARDINIÈRES, PEDESTALS, &c.

No. 35.
Flower Pot in Ivory Ware,
decorated in natural colours
and Gilt. 2s. 6d.

No. 31.
Flower Pot in natural
colours on Ivory Ware
and Gilt.
1s. 9d. each.

Embossed Pedestal and Flower Pot
in Bronze Green, or Deep Yellow
Glaze. 4 ft. high.
Complete £2 12 6

Pedestal and Flower Pot of similar
style. 3 ft. 8 in. high.
Complete £1 15 0

Minton's Art Ware.
10½ in. diameter.
3s. 9d. each.

No. 37.
Flower Pot 7 in. high, Ivory
ground, colored Flowers
and Gilt.
1s. 9d. each.

Majolica Heron, with recep-
tacle for growing Plant
or Palm.

15 in. high	.. £0 15	0
23 in. „	.. 2 2	0
27 in. „	.. 3 10	0
32 in. „	.. 4 10	0

Dwarf Pedestal and Pot,
in shaded art colours,
28 in. high.
Complete 17s. 6d.

Minton Jardinière, on
Dwarf Pedestal.
20½ in. high.
Complete 18s. 6d.

Majolica Stork, with re-
ceptacle for growing
Plant or Palm.

15 in. high	.. £0 15	0
23 in. „	.. 2 2	0
27 in. „	.. 3 10	0
32 in. „	.. 4 10	0

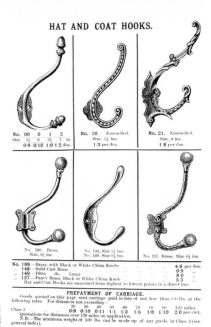

HAT AND COAT HOOKS.

No. 00	0	1	2
Size 5½	6	6¼	7 in.
0.9	0/10	1/0	1/2 doz.

No. 20.—Enamelled.
Size, 5½ ins.
1/3 per doz.

No. 21.—Enamelled.
Size, 8 ins.
1 8 per doz.

No. 189, Brass,
Size, 6½ ins.

No. 148, Size 5½ ins.
No. 149, Size 6½ ins.

No. 137. Brass. Size 6½ ins.

No. 189.—Brass, with Black or White China Knobs ... ... 4.6 per doz.
„ 148.—Solid Cast Brass ... ... 6.9 „
„ 149.—Ditto do. Large ... ... 8.0 „
„ 137.—Fancy Brass, Black or White China Knob ... ... 5.3 „
Hat and Coat Hooks are measured from highest to lowest points in a direct line.

PREPAYMENT OF CARRIAGE.

Goods quoted on this page sent carriage paid in lots of not less than 500 lbs. at the following rates. For distances not exceeding—

Class 3	20	30	40	50	60	70	80	90	120 miles.
	0.9	0/10	0/11	1/1	1/3	1/5	1/6	1/10	2.0 per cwt.

Quotations for distances over 120 miles on application.
N.B.—The minimum weight of 500 lbs. can be made up of any goods in Class 3 (see general index).

BADDA 697

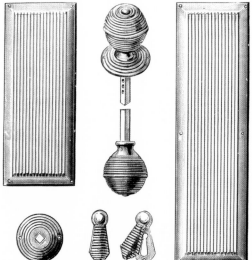

DOOR FURNITURE—Continued.
Brass Furniture for Mortice and Rim Locks.

BADDA 697

No. 5.—Brass Furniture and Finger Plates, Queen Anne Style, with Screw through Spindles.

ILLUSTRATION 5
Catalogue for O'Brien, Thomas & Co, 1893

ILLUSTRATION 4 Houseplants were a feature of many late-Victorian homes. Ferns and palms were particularly popular, especially in halls and living rooms. Many ornate jardinières and pedestals were available.

ILLUSTRATION 5 At the time, all men wore hats. A wooden stand or a series of hat and coat hooks in the hall was therefore necessary.

ILLUSTRATION 6 Suites of door furniture - handles, finger plates and keyhole covers – were available in a variety of styles and finishes. This ribbed brass set is in an eighteenth-century style.

ILLUSTRATION 6
Catalogue for O'Brien, Thomas & Co, 1893

ILLUSTRATION 7

Drawing room in Putney, London, 1907

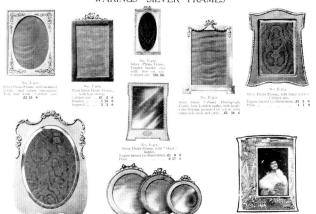

WARINGS' SILVER FRAMES

BADDA 96

ILLUSTRATION 8

Catalogue for Waring & Gillow, about 1907

ILLUSTRATION 7 This 1900s London drawing room is light and spacious, as were the most fashionable interiors at this time. It has little furniture, few ornaments or pictures, simple window treatments and a white ceiling and walls. Pattern is confined to the wide frieze and loose chintz covers.

ILLUSTRATION 8 Family photographs were proudly displayed on shelves, tables, pianos and mantelpieces. These silver frames indicate some of choices available in th 1900s.

ILLUSTRATION 9 Dinner, dessert, tea and breakfast services were always patterned.

BADDA 1

ILLUSTRATION 9

Catalogue for Osler's, 1910

ILLUSTRATION 10

Catalogue for Liberty's, 1910

No. 1. Candlesticks.
3¾ ins. high.
10/6

No. 2. Candlesticks.
6½ ins. diameter, 1½ ins. high.
10/6

No. 3. Candlesticks.
5¼ ins. high.
7/6

No. 4. Cake Trays.
9¼ ins. long.
12/6

No. 5. Candlesticks.
9 ins. high.
17/6

No. 6. Biscuit Boxes.
4½ ins. square.
£1 . 1 . 0

No. 7. Flower Vases.
With glass lining.
6½ ins. high.
14/6

No. 8. Hot Milk Glass
Holders (complete).
8/6

No. 9. Cake Baskets.
9¼ by 6½ ins.
15/6

No. 10. Hot Water Jugs.
With cane handle.
Capacity 1¾ pints.
£1 . 2 . 6

BADDA 355

ILLUSTRATION 10 Arts-and-Crafts-inspired 'Cymric' silverware and 'Tudric' pewterware were sold by Liberty's in large quantities in the 1900s.

KITCHENS

The late-Victorian and Edwardian middle-class kitchen was not a public space. Visitors never went there. It was treated as a service area, a place for servants. Consequently, little interest was paid to it decoratively. It was only when the problem of finding and keeping servants grew more acute, at the turn of the century, that the comfort and convenience of the kitchen received any attention.

Virtually every kitchen had a coal-burning, cast-iron range for cooking and heating water. By the 1900s, freestanding gas stoves were on sale but they were still unusual and were often used alongside a range.

Storage was provided in fitted cupboards and a wooden dresser with open shelving on which china was displayed. Pots and pans were either kept in the cupboards below or visible on shelving and hooks. A large central wooden table was used for food preparation, sometimes with a cool marble top for pastry making. Tiled larders with wooden or marble shelves were included for food storage.

In the early 1890s there was usually a scullery attached to the kitchen. This was where the wet and dirty work, such as washing up and food preparation, took place. But in the twentieth century, new houses were increasingly built without sculleries, their functions being absorbed into the kitchen. Sinks were large and square, made either of white porcelain or stoneware. To the side was a grooved, sloping wooden draining board and there was a wooden plate rack on the wall above the sink.

Furniture was more functional than decorative. Linoleum flooring and washable paint were practical and easy to clean. Scullery floors were usually tiled or sometimes of stone. The ceiling was washed or whitewashed every year. Kitchen walls were usually painted cream or green but were still divided by adding rails and friezes. Washable sanitary wallpapers were also used.

ILLUSTRATION I
Catalogue for Waring & Gillow, about 1910

ILLUSTRATION I Cupboards, dressers and shelves were built into alcoves and recesses to save space and cleaning. Although this is a well-equipped kitchen, the decoration and furniture is basic. The crockery on the dressers, the patterned linoleum, the sanitary wallpaper and the geranium on the window ledge give it a simple, homely air.

ILLUSTRATION 2

Catalogue for O'Brien, Thomas & Co, 1893

THE No. 3 O'BRIEN EXCHANGE KITCHENER.
(REGISTERED TITLE.)

BADDA 697

ILLUSTRATION 2 A cast-iron kitchen range was found in almost every kitchen. Available in several sizes, suitable for different households, 'kitcheners' all included at least one oven, a hob and perhaps a warming oven. Some had tiled surrounds to the hob. Fuelled by coal, they were used to heat water as well as to cook and required constant work and attention to keep them going.

THE DAVIS GAS STOVE Co Ltd.

The Metropolitan

No 10

LONDON

These Stoves may be inspected at our

City Show Rooms, 59, Queen Victoria St., E.C.

And can be hired from all London Gas Companies and most of those in the Provinces, at

LOW QUARTERLY RENTALS.

Apply for all particulars and for a FREE COOKERY BOOK to:—

METROPOLITAN ENGINEERING WORKS, Camberwell, LONDON, S.E.

BACDA 2357

ILLUSTRATION 3

Madge's Book of Cookery, about 1902

ILLUSTRATION 3 Freestanding gas stoves were expensive, fairly basic and not widely used. Providing virtually instantaneous energy for cooking, they were particularly useful in the summer, using less fuel and keeping the kitchen cooler than the kitchen range.

ILLUSTRATION 4 Traditional cast-iron kitchen scales had a series of weights and a brass weighing-pan.

BACDA 1164

Best Quality "Registered" Weighing Machine.
4 lbs. down ... ... 12s. 6d.
7 " " ... ... 15s. 0d.
14 " " ... ... 18s. 9d.
Second Quality, with loose weights 7s. 6d., 8s. 6d., 9s. 6d. complete

ILLUSTRATION 4

Catalogue for Oetzmann's, about 1890

BATHROOMS

By the turn of the century, a bathroom was a middle-class necessity and by 1910, bathrooms were present in all new urban middle-class houses in Britain. Progress was slower in rural areas due to the reduced availability of mains drainage.

The first plumbed-in baths had been in the houses of the very wealthy and usually had wooden surrounds, as if they were pieces of furniture. They were often located in a dressing room next to the bedroom and these bathrooms were decorated not unlike the bedrooms.

But by about 1900, bathrooms had become important in the fight against dirt and disease in the home and their design changed accordingly, to reflect their functionality. Britain now led Europe in bathroom design. Fittings were required to demonstrate cleanliness. Wooden surrounds were therefore avoided. Baths became freestanding, with exposed legs, to ensure every surface could be reached for cleaning. Hand basins were supplied on plain metal or ceramic legs, rather than in wooden cabinets or on highly decorative cast-iron stands. There was usually a mirror above the hand basin and perhaps a toothbrush holder. White ceramic surfaces for fittings were far less ornate than those available in the 1890s.

If there was a shower, it could be fitted over the bath or in a separate unit with a porcelain or marble base and a waterproof curtain or semi-circular zinc surround. A large showerhead ensured a complete drenching. A flush toilet was generally located in a separate room. Nickel-plated or silver-plated bronze taps, easier to clean than brass, were popular.

Walls could be tiled, at least to dado height, or painted in a washable paint. There were washable, varnished sanitary wallpapers in tile designs and special decorative friezes. Plain or unobtrusively patterned linoleum was a common floor covering. Tiles or cork carpet squares were alternatives.

ILLUSTRATION 1 Late-nineteenth-century plumbed-in baths had flat top edges and were enclosed in a wooden casing. This example was available either with a walnut or mahogany surround, a choice of taps and an imitation sienna marble interior.

ILLUSTRATION 2 Cast-iron washstands, known as lavatory stands, were fixed to the wall. They were thought to harbour less dirt than those enclosed in wooden cases. Ornate decoration was common until the early 1900s. A gold-leafed version of this washstand was available.

ILLUSTRATION 1
Catalogue for Oetzmann's, about 1890

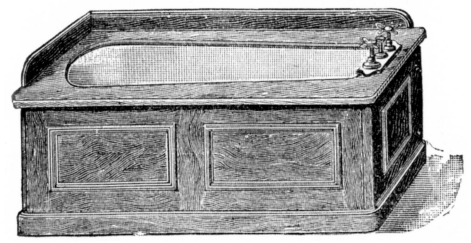

BADDA 1/64

ILLUSTRATION 2

Catalogue for O'Brien, Thomas & Co, 1893

ILLUSTRATION 3

Catalogue for O'Brien, Thomas & Co, 1893

BADDA 697

BADDA 697

ILLUSTRATION 3 In the early part of the period, elaborate toilet bowls complete with intricate metal wall brackets were popular. They came supplied with wooden toilet seats but without a lid.

ILLUSTRATION 4

Catalogue for O'Brien, Thomas & Co, 1893

THE "TRENT" SANITARY CLOSET.
For use either as Closet, Urinal or Slop Sink.

BADDA 697

ILLUSTRATION 4 High-level water closets with exposed pipe work and long toilet chains were the norm. Plainer toilet bowls were also available in the 1890s. Such designs worked well with the simpler fittings, which sold well in the 1900s.

ILLUSTRATION 5

Catalogue for Hampton's, about 1910

ILLUSTRATION 5 This is a later example and it shows the plainer fittings that were popular at the time. The freestanding roll-top bath has clawed feet. Until 1910, when improved heat-resistant paints became available, enamelled cast-iron baths needed continual repainting. Wall tiling was practical and hygienic but an expensive option. Where walls were completely tiled, they were arranged to create distinct dado and upper wall areas. Coloured tiles made the room less clinical. Heated towel rails were on sale or towels could be hung from a roller behind the door or a rod fixed to the wall. The only moveable bathroom furniture was a chair, usually with a cork seat.

FURTHER READING

Edwardian House Style Hilary Hockman (1994)

Living Rooms – 20th-Century Interiors at the Geffrye Museum Lesley Hoskins (1998)

Silver Studio of design: a design and sourcebook for home decoration Mark Turner and Lesley Hoskins (1995)

The Edwardian House Helen Long (1993)

Victorian and Edwardian Furniture and Interiors Jeremy Cooper (1998)

PLACES TO VISIT

MoDA (Museum of Domestic Design & Architecture), Middlesex University, Cat Hill, Barnet, Hertfordshire EN4 8HT Telephone 020 8411 5244 www.moda.mdx.ac.uk MoDA's permanent exhibition, *Exploring Interiors: Decoration of the Home 1900-1960*, includes a section on 1900-1915. Its extensive collections of turn-of-the-century trade catalogues, home magazines, designs, wallpapers and textiles can be viewed by appointment in MoDA's study room.

BLACKWELL, Bowness-on-Windermere, Cumbria LA23 3JR Telephone 01539 446139 www.blackwell.org.uk Blackwell was designed by the Arts and Crafts architect M H Bailie Scott as a holiday home for Sir Edward Holt. Completed in 1900, much of its interior decoration has survived intact.

GEFFRYE MUSEUM, Kingsland Road, London E2 8EA Telephone 020 7739 9893 www.geffrye-museum.org.uk The museum displays include a drawing and living hall in a new London suburban house of about 1910.

MR STRAW'S HOUSE, 7 Blyth Grove, Worksop, Nottinghamshire S81 0JG Telephone 01909 482380 www.nationaltrust.org.uk The interior of this modest semi-detached Edwardian house is unaltered since the 1930s and features Victorian furniture and household objects. It is a National Trust property.

SHAW'S CORNER, Ayot St Lawrence, Near Welwyn, Hertfordshire AL6 9BX Telephone 01438 820307 www.nationaltrust.org.uk/regions/thameschilterns An Edwardian villa, the home of George Bernard Shaw from 1906 until his death in 1950. The interior is set out as it was in his lifetime. It is a National Trust property.

STANDEN, West Hoathly Road, East Grinstead, Sussex RH19 4NE Telephone 01342 323029 www.nationaltrust.org.uk A family house completed in 1894 by the architect and friend of William Morris, Philip Webb. Now a National Trust property, it is a showpiece of the Arts and Crafts movement and also has many of its original electric light fittings.

THE TENEMENT HOUSE, 145 Buccleuch Street, Garnethill, Glasgow G3 6QN Telephone 0141 333 0183 www.nts.org.uk A first-floor typical late-Victorian Glasgow tenement apartment retaining most of its original features, including a kitchen range, brass bedstead and tiled cast-iron fireplace and overmantel. It is a National Trust for Scotland property.

MoDA is known as the 'museum of the history of the home'. Its varied exhibitions give a vivid picture of domestic life during the first half of the twentieth century whilst also looking at contemporary design and other issues related to the domestic environment.

Gallery talks, events, practical workshops and study days provide educational, informative and entertaining experiences for adults and children.

MoDA holds six collections and a dedicated Study Room allows access to items not on display.

SILVER STUDIO COLLECTION

The archive of a commercial pattern design practice active between 1880 and 1963. Its many thousands of designs, wallpapers and textile samples span the popular styles of the period.

CROWN WALLPAPER COLLECTION

Wallpaper books mainly from the 1950s, represent the colourful and engaging patterns of that time.

DOMESTIC DESIGN COLLECTION

More than 4,000 books, magazines and trade catalogues relating to design for the home and household management (1850-1960).

SIR JM RICHARDS LIBRARY

Books and journals collected by Sir JM Richards (1907-1992), a leading architectural writer. The collection covers architecture, interiors, furniture, landscape and town planning.

PEGGY ANGUS ARCHIVE

The entire contents of the London studio of Peggy Angus (1904-1993), an artist, teacher and designer of tiles and bespoke hand-printed wallpapers.

CHARLES HASLER COLLECTION

An archive relating to the work of Charles Hasler (1908-1992), a typographer and graphic designer who played a significant role in many high-profile exhibitions, poster campaigns and in book publishing from the mid-1930s to the mid-1980s.